Silly
Scenarios
For
Silly
Kids

(Would you rather?)

D0367853

by Silly Willy

How to play!

Out of the choices you must choose
one of the answers!

An example,

Would you rather:

be a dog or

–or–

be a cat?

If you would prefer to be a dog rather
than a cat, you would choose the first
option: be a dog. But the choices in this
book are not all this easy!

And remember, you must choose!

Even if it is still **not** an ideal scenario! If
you cannot decide, imagine the GOOD
and BAD sides of each option!

Good Luck!

Would You Rather:

...be a pirate -or- a Viking?

Would You Rather:

...be able to speak all languages

-or-

live in a castle?

...have hands instead of feet

-or-

feet instead of hands?

...fly or

-or-

turn invisible?

Would You Rather:

...be a friendly ghost

-or-

a scary monster?

Would You Rather:

...travel through space on a skateboard

-or-

travel through time on a jet ski?

Would You Rather:

...own a crime-fighting **police dog**
-or-
own a crime-fighting **hotdog**?

Would You Rather:

...scream your name when you
introduce yourself

-or-

always misspell your own name?

...have fingers twice as long as
they are now

-or-

half as short?

...be good at school work

-or-

good at climbing trees?

Would You Rather:

...know your future

-or-

know what other people are thinking?

...have the nose of a pig

-or-

the butt of a pig?

Would You Rather:

...have all your food taste like
rotten fish

-or-

have your clothes made of rotten fish?

...be able to talk to animals

-or-

be able to control people's legs?

...meet a superhero's sidekick

-or-

be a super villain?

Would You Rather:

...like the smell of smelly feet

-or-

like the smell of rotting fish?

...have great hair and
terrible clothes

-or-

terrible hair and great clothes?

...excel at math

-or-

excel at English?

Would You Rather:

...have a big head

-or-

a small body?

Would You Rather:

...eat as much pizza-flavored
ice cream as possible

-or-

eat as much ice cream-topped
pizza as possible?

...invent a new food

-or-

make a type of food disappear forever?

...eat sludge for dinner

-or-

eat sludge for breakfast?

Would You Rather:

...be stuck on a remote island with plenty of food

-or-

be stuck on a boat with no food?

~~~~~~~~~~~~~

...laugh when others cry

-or-

cry when others laugh?

~~~~~~~~~~~~~

...be really tall

-or-

really short?

Would You Rather:

...kiss all the people you meet
-or-
kiss all the pets you meet?

Would You Rather:

...have your head on backwards

-or-

your butt on the front?

~~~~~~~~~~~~~

...only wear cut-off jeans

-or-

only wear jeans that go up to your chest?

~~~~~~~~~~~~~

...wear oversized hats in winter

-or-

thick sweaters in summer?

Would You Rather:

...skydive from a bus

-or-

skydive from outer space?

~~~~~~~~~~~~~

...have no control of your legs

-or-

no control of the volume of your voice?

~~~~~~~~~~~~~

...stay the same age forever

-or-

every year be a random age?

Would You Rather:

...be able to jump tall buildings

-or-

walk up the sides of tall buildings?

Would You Rather:

...be a famous singer who cannot dance

-or-

a famous actor who is camera shy?

...be attacked by a dragon

-or-

attacked by a swarm of flying worms?

...live in a world without TV

-or-

live in a world without roads?

Would You Rather:

...be someone's beloved pet

-or-

have a naughty pet unicorn?

...have a fear of flying

-or-

a fear of swimming?

...be able to play every musical instrument

-or-

invent a new instrument?

Would You Rather:

...be this guy

–or–

be this guy?

Would You Rather:

...always be 10 minutes late

-or-

always be on time but never wearing pants?

~~~~~~~~~~~~

...be smart

-or-

popular?

~~~~~~~~~~~~

...have an extra arm

-or-

an extra mouth?

Would You Rather:

...have feathers as hands

-or-

hoofs as feet?

...be locked inside a toy store

-or-

a theme park?

...travel through time without ever
knowing what year it is

-or-

travel through time as the world's
most wanted criminal?

Would You Rather:

...have a nosy sister

-or-

a bully brother?

~~~~~~~~~

...have a bath with a hungry shark

-or-

be thrown into space by an elephant?

~~~~~~~~~

...your voice sound like a duck

-or-

everyone else sound like a duck?

Would You Rather:

...forget to wear pants

–or–

forget your age?

Would You Rather:

...be an astronaut who is scared
of the dark

-or-

a pilot who is scared of heights?

~~~~~~~~

...time travel forward in time

-or-

time travel backwards in time?

~~~~~~~~

...have a mouthful of jellybeans

-or-

a mouthful of gold?

Would You Rather:

...be a cartoon character
-or-
a professional wrestler?

~~~~~~

...have a photographic memory
-or-
never forget what you were told?

~~~~~~

...have boogers on your face
-or-
kiss someone with boogers
on their face?

Would You Rather:

...shoot lasers from your eyes

-or-

draw rainbows with your fingers?

Would You Rather:

...listen to only country music

-or-

only be able to talk like a cowboy?

...only be allowed to sleep for one hour
a day

-or-

only be allowed to get out of your bed
for one hour a day?

...wear a wrestling costume

-or-

wear a mascot costume?

Would You Rather:

...only eat spinach for 3 months straight

-or-

only eat cabbage ice cream for
3 months straight?

...dance in public for 30 minutes

-or-

dance in private for 5 hours?

...have your food look like vomit

-or-

taste like rotten eggs?

Would You Rather:

...dance like this

-or-

dance like this?

Would You Rather:

...own every comic ever made

-or-

own every video game ever made?

...be great at playing drums

-or-

great at singing?

...live in a house made of spider webs

-or-

live in a house made of used tissues?

Would You Rather:

...as a superhero, wear a cape

-or-

wear a mask?

--- ~~~~~~ ---

...have chewing gum stuck in your hair

-or-

a huge dribble stain on your shirt?

--- ~~~~~~ ---

...know that one of your friends is
an alien

-or-

know which family member has
hidden treasure?

Would You Rather:

... be scared of the sun

-or-

be scared of shadows?

Would You Rather:

...be a powerful king

-or-

the world's greatest gamer?

~~~~~~~~~~~~

...be able to read lips

-or-

be able to impersonate TV characters?

~~~~~~~~~~~~

...kiss your crush

-or-

crush the highest score on your favorite game?

Would You Rather:

...achieve the highest scores on school
tests without studying

-or-

never have a detention?

~~~~~~~~~~~~~~~~~~~~~~~~~

...have an orchestra follow you and play
music based on your actions
(like a movie)

-or-

have some consistently narrating
your day (like a book)?

Would You Rather:

...float away when windy

–or–

sink into soft ground when raining?

Would You Rather:

...silence an arguing sister

-or-

freeze an annoying brother?

...always be fun to be around

-or-

always be correct?

...have very neat handwriting

-or-

never make a mess?

Would You Rather:

...see through walls

-or-

walk through walls?

Would You Rather:

...have no one ever complete your high
five

-or-

when you high five, you must
scream out *"Bonza!"*?

~~~~~~~~~~~~~~~~

...hear the rumors about you

-or-

start rumors about yourself?

~~~~~~~~~~~~~~~~

...be followed by a ghost

-or-

follow a ghost into a haunted house?

Would You Rather:

...be really good at magic tricks

-or-

be really good at spoiling magic tricks?

Would You Rather:

...complete an important exam with a
short, blunt pencil

-or-

write every letter of your answers with
a different color?

~~~~~~~~~~

...wear your hat backwards for the
rest of your life

-or-

slippers as shoes for the
rest of your life?

Would You Rather:

...know a secret about your
grandparents

-or-

keep a secret from them?

...teach science at your school

-or-

be part of a dangerous
science experiment?

Would You Rather:

...find a spider in your underwear

-or-

find a spider in your ear?

Would You Rather:

...see everything in a shade of yellow

-or-

hear everything in a high pitch?

...collect rare coins

-or-

ridiculous hats?

...eat the cat's food

-or-

the dog's food?

Would You Rather:

...be stranded on a remote island
for 1 year

-or-

be locked up in a bathroom for 1 year?

Would You Rather:

...be a twin

-or-

have a twin?

...discover that toilet paper is bad
for you

-or-

discover candy makes you smarter?

...invite only animals to your birthday
party

-or-

invite only the cool school teachers?

Would You Rather:

...discover that you are an
imaginary friend

-or-

discover that your imaginary friend
doesn't like you?

~~~~~~~~~~~~~~~~~~~~~~

...have fingers emerge from your
nose when eating

-or-

knives and forks emerge from your
nose when eating?

Would You Rather:

...control an army of robots

−or−

be a robot?

Would You Rather:

...cut your own hair

–or–

have a chimp with scissors cut it?

...give everyone bad advice

–or–

always receive bad advice?

...swap faces with someone else

–or–

or swap bodies?

Would You Rather:

...eat the hottest chili in the world

-or-

walk through a field of poison
ivy naked?

...tightrope across a canyon with
no wind blowing

-or-

tightrope 30 feet above the ground
in windy conditions?

Would You Rather:

...be caught picking your nose

-or-

be caught cheating on a test?

Would You Rather:

...your favorite school teacher
move schools

-or-

your worst school teacher move
in with you?

～～～～～～～～

...the school principal visit you on
vacation to deliver homework

-or-

clean the school grounds naked?

Would You Rather:

...tell your classmates what you
think of them

-or-

tell everyone your worst secret
at the school assembly?

... visit the vet when you are sick

-or-

visit a chocolate factory when
you are sick?

Would You Rather:

...your school bus be a hotrod

-or-

a hovercraft?

...look like a bird

-or-

sound like a bird?

Would You Rather:

...be the smartest in your classroom

-or-

be the smartest in your family?

...be in the same grade as your Mom

-or-

be in the same grade as your Dad?

...live inside your school

-or-

live 2 hours away from school?

Would You Rather:

...change your name to
'Turbo Power'

-or-

or change your name to
'Lightning Strike'?

...be a judge on a game show

-or-

a judge in the courtroom?

Would You Rather:

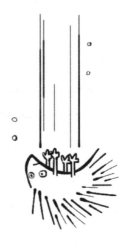

...catch a falling porcupine

–or–

pat an angry lion?

Would You Rather:

...fall off a swing

-or-

fall off a trampoline?

...have a best friend with magic powers

-or-

a best friend who never lied to you?

...control the clouds

-or-

control the wind?

Would You Rather:

...have painful, blistering sunburn

-or-

be freezing, shivering cold?

~~~~~~

...only listen to rap music

-or-

country music?

~~~~~~

...swim in a tub of hot sauce

-or-

lick yogurt off your sister's face?

Would You Rather:

...be a *brightly-colored* ninja

−or−

be a *noisy* ninja?

Would You Rather:

...climb an Egyptian pyramid

-or-

live as an Egyptian pharaoh?

...sleep in a bed of snakes

-or-

sleep in a bed of mosquitoes?

...this book taste like bubble gum

-or-

this book smell like bubble gum?

Would You Rather:

...keep your current school year
the same

-or-

stay awake at school until you learn
the content and have the rest
of the year off?

...sit in a rocket not knowing
where it will go

-or-

ride a bicycle with no brakes downhill?

Would You Rather:

...breathe fire like a dragon

-or-

when you speak, **comic speech balloons** appear?

Would You Rather:

...be able to move things
with your mind

-or-

be able to throw a tennis ball
around the planet?

...see in the dark

-or-

glow in the dark?

...wet the bed for a week

-or-

dress as a belly dancer for a week?

Would You Rather:

...name your school

-or-

have your school named after you?

...live in a world of fairy tales
and castles

-or-

live in a world of sci-fi and aliens?

...commentate the football on live TV

-or-

be a referee in the Super Bowl?

Would You Rather:

...be the funniest person in the world
-or-
be the strongest person in the world?

...always be yelling
-or-
always be whispering?

Would You Rather:

...have food stuck in your teeth when
talking to your school crush

-or-

your crush sneezes and covers
you with snot?

...own a slow camel

-or-

a fast tortoise?

...be great at making witty one-liners

-or-

communicate by pulling faces so you
don't need to talk?

Would You Rather:

...be unable to understand how
a door works

-or-

believe mirrors are actually windows?

...have a movie made of your life

-or-

write, direct and star in your
own movie?

Would You Rather:

...go to a school where no one
speaks English

-or-

go to a school where the
teachers are zombies?

Would You Rather:

...run with scissors blindfolded

-or-

run around an active volcano?

Silly Situations!

Come up with some crazy answers for the following **silly questions!** Compare your answers with your friends and family!

To make it more challenging, yell out the first answer that comes to mind!

And remember, the **sillier** the better!

Good Luck!

Silly Situations!

If you only had **one song** stuck in your head for the rest of your life what would it be?

~~~~~~~~~~~~

If you could have a *superpower*, what would it be?

~~~~~~~~~~~~

If you could be an animal, what animal would you be?

~~~~~~~~~~~~

If you could only eat one meal for the **rest of your life**, what meal would you choose?

Silly Situations!

If you had the power to create a law, what **law** would you create?

~~~~~~~~~~~~~~~~~~~~~~~~

If you could put **anything** in your room, what would you choose?

~~~~~~~~~~~~~~~~~~~~~~~~

Who would be your arch-enemy if they were from a **movie**?

~~~~~~~~~~~~~~~~~~~~~~~~

If you needed to change your name to a name of a **country**, what name would you chose?

Silly Situations!

If you could move your **classroom**,
where would you move it?

If you could meet anyone from **history**,
who would you like to meet?

If you time travelled and were **never**
able to return, where would you go?

If you could go bowling with a **cartoon**,
who would it be?

Silly Situations!

Who would you choose to be stranded
on an island with?

~~~~~~~~~~~~~~~~~~~~~~~

If you wrote a **famous book**, what
would you name the title?

~~~~~~~~~~~~~~~~~~~~~~~

If you were able to make a movie about
anything, what would it be about?

~~~~~~~~~~~~~~~~~~~~~~~

What would you do if a **volcano**
erupted in your bedroom?

Silly Situations!

Where would you go if could fly a
jumbo jet?

―――――――――――――

If you could paint your family car, what
color would you paint it?

―――――――――――――

What would you do if you discovered a
monster *really* did live under your bed?

―――――――――――――

What would you do if you suddenly
could not talk?

Silly Situations!

What would you do if you woke up tomorrow and your legs had **doubled** in length?

~~~~~~~~~~

What would you do if your hair suddenly turned **glowing pink**?

~~~~~~~~~~

If you could make up a **language**, what would it be called?

~~~~~~~~~~

If you could be the **world champion** of a sport, what sport would it be?

Silly Situations!

How would you survive if all your **food** floated away?

～～～～～～

If fictional characters were **real**, who would be your best friend?

～～～～～～

What do you see being the **biggest advantage** if you were made of concrete?

～～～～～～

What do you see being the **biggest disadvantage** if you were made of butter?

And finally,
Would You Rather:

eat your boogers

-or-

....not?

~~~~~~~~~~~~~~~~~

The End

Also Available:

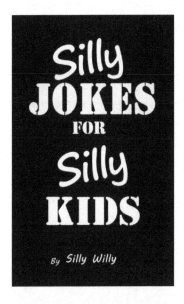

Made in the USA
Middletown, DE
11 November 2019